THE BOOK OF DIGNITY

Alfonso Borello

Villaggio Publishing Ltd

CONTENTS

PREFACE

Cicero, a Roman statesman and philosopher, wrote extensively on the concept of dignity in the 1st century BCE. He believed that dignity was an inherent quality of human beings and the foundation of human rights. In his writings, he emphasized the importance of dignity in ensuring that individuals were treated justly and fairly. Cicero's ideas on dignity had a significant influence on later thinkers, including Kant and other Enlightenment philosophers. His writings also played a role in shaping the development of international human rights law.

As the author of this book on the subject of dignity, I feel deeply passionate about exploring the various dimensions of this complex and nuanced concept. Throughout my career, I have encountered countless examples of the ways in which human dignity has been both affirmed and violated, and it is my belief that a deeper understanding of this concept is critical to promoting justice and equality in our world. In writing this book, my goal is to provide readers with a comprehensive and accessible overview of the philosophical and practical implications of dignity. Drawing on a wide range of sources, from historical texts to contemporary social justice movements, I aim to highlight the many ways in which dignity has been and continues to be a driving force in our collective struggle for human rights and dignity.

Throughout the pages of this book, I will explore the role of dignity in various fields, including healthcare, criminal justice, and social policy, and examine the challenges and limitations of applying this concept in practice. I will also analyze the ways in which social injustices can undermine human dignity, and discuss the ongoing importance of promoting dignity as a means of addressing structural inequalities. Ultimately, my hope is that this book will inspire readers to engage more deeply with the concept of dignity, and to work towards a world in which all individuals are afforded the respect and recognition that they deserve.

EARLY WORK ON DIGNITY

The concept of dignity has been present throughout human history, and there is no one definitive answer to what the very first written work on dignity was. However, one of the earliest known discussions of dignity can be found in the works of the ancient Greek philosophers, particularly Aristotle and Plato. They wrote extensively about the importance of respecting the inherent worth and value of all human beings, regardless of their social status or circumstances.

Another early text that touches on the concept of dignity is the Code of Hammurabi, a set of laws created by the Babylonian king Hammurabi in the 18th century BCE. The code contains provisions for the fair and just treatment of all people, and emphasizes the importance of respecting individual dignity and autonomy.

Overall, while there is no one specific text that can be considered the very first written work on dignity, the concept has been a part of human discourse for thousands of years and can be found in many different cultures and traditions.

THE IMPORTANCE OF DIGNITY

Dignity is not just an abstract concept. It's a feeling that resides within each one of us, a sense of worth and value that we all carry with us throughout our lives. When we are treated with dignity, we feel respected, valued, and validated. When our dignity is violated, we feel demeaned, dehumanized, and degraded. Dignity is not just a philosophical concept, it's an emotional experience that is at the core of what it means to be human.

Think about a time when you felt your dignity was violated. Perhaps someone spoke to you disrespectfully or treated you as if you were inferior. How did it make you feel? Maybe you felt angry, frustrated, or humiliated. Whatever the emotion, the violation of your dignity likely left you feeling hurt and diminished. Now think about a time when you were treated with dignity. Maybe someone acknowledged your efforts or showed you gratitude for something you had done. How did that make you feel? Probably appreciated, respected, and valued. The contrast between these two experiences demonstrates the profound impact that dignity can have on our emotional wellbeing.

The recognition and protection of human dignity is the foundation of human rights, and the lack of respect for human dignity is at the root of many of the world's most pressing social problems. Consider the ongoing struggle for racial justice in the United States. Racism is a violation of human dignity, as it reduces individuals to their skin color and denies them the full respect and recognition that they deserve as human beings. The same can be said for other forms of discrimination, such as sexism, ableism, and homophobia. These forms of discrimination are all rooted in a denial of human dignity, and they contribute to the perpetuation of social and economic inequality.

The fight for human dignity is not just a political or social struggle, it is a deeply personal one. It is a fight to be recognized and valued for who we are, regardless of our race, gender, sexual orientation, or any other characteristic. It is a fight to be treated with respect and kindness, to have our contributions acknowledged and appreciated, and to be given the opportunity to fulfill our potential as human beings.

Jean-Paul Sartre had a unique perspective on the concept of dignity. He believed that dignity is a subjective concept and that each individual is responsible for creating their own sense of dignity through their actions and choices. Sartre argued that we are all born into a world that is inherently meaningless and that we must create our own sense of purpose and value through our choices and actions. In this way, dignity is something that we must actively create for ourselves, rather than something that is inherent or given to us by society.

Sartre also believed that dignity is intimately connected to freedom and choice. He argued that we can only truly be dignified when we are free to make our own choices and act according to our own values and beliefs.

DIFFERENT RELIGIONS HAVE VARYING VIEWS ON DIGNITY

Here are a few examples:

Christianity: Christianity teaches that all human beings are created in the image of God and have inherent dignity and worth. Christians are called to treat others with respect and compassion, regardless of their background or status.

Islam: In Islam, dignity is closely tied to the concept of "karamah," or honor. Muslims believe that every person has inherent dignity and that it is the responsibility of the community to ensure that this dignity is respected and upheld.

Judaism: Judaism teaches that all human beings are created in the image of God and therefore have inherent dignity and worth. Jews are called to treat others with respect and compassion, regardless of their background or status.

Hinduism: In Hinduism, dignity is closely linked to the concept of "ahimsa," or nonviolence. Hindus believe that every person has inherent dignity and that it is the responsibility of individuals and society as a whole to respect and protect this dignity.

Buddhism: Buddhism teaches that all human beings have inherent dignity and worth and that this should be respected and upheld. Buddhists are called to treat others with compassion and to work towards reducing suffering in the world.

THE CONCEPT OF DIGNITY IN CINEMA

Neo-realism was a film movement that emerged in Italy after World War II. It focused on the lives of ordinary people and aimed to capture the social and economic realities of post-war Italy. Many of the films produced during this movement dealt with themes of poverty, social injustice, and human dignity.

The concept of dignity is a central theme in neo-realism movies. These films often depict characters who are struggling to maintain their dignity in the face of poverty and social inequality. For example, in the classic neo-realist film "Bicycle Thieves," the protagonist Antonio struggles to find work and support his family. When his bicycle, which he needs for his job, is stolen, he sets out on a desperate search to recover it, risking his own dignity in the process.

In neo-realism films, dignity is often portrayed as something that is fragile and easily lost. Characters must fight to maintain their dignity in the face of adversity and injustice, and their struggles are often portrayed as heroic acts of resistance against oppressive systems.

Overall, neo-realism movies offer a powerful reflection on the concept of dignity, highlighting the importance of human dignity in the face of social and economic struggles. Unfortunately, as often as natures dictates, and contrary to the poetic of Aristotle, the story has a beginning, a middle, and end, but no denouement, or emotional release.

The idea of human dignity has a long and rich history, spanning across philosophical and religious traditions. It has been explored by some of the most influential thinkers in history, from Aristotle and Cicero to Immanuel Kant and Friedrich Nietzsche. In recent times, it has been enshrined in international human rights law as a cornerstone of human rights and a universal value.

MACHIAVELLI ON DIGNITY

Niccolò Machiavelli, the Italian political philosopher of the Renaissance period, had a unique perspective on the concept of dignity. In his most famous work, "The Prince," Machiavelli argues that a leader must prioritize the stability and security of the state over any notions of personal morality or dignity.

Machiavelli saw rulers as having two options: to be loved or to be feared. He argued that being loved was ideal, but being feared was often necessary in order to maintain power and stability. He believed that a ruler must sometimes act in ways that may be considered cruel or immoral in order to preserve the well-being of the state.

In this context, the concept of dignity takes on a different meaning. For Machiavelli, dignity was not a universal human right, but a quality that rulers must project in order to command respect and loyalty from their subjects. He argued that a ruler must appear dignified and strong in order to maintain their power, even if this meant acting in ways that may be considered ruthless or oppressive.

Overall, Machiavelli's perspective on dignity highlights the tension between personal morality and the practical considerations of political leadership. His work continues to be studied and debated by political scientists and philosophers today, and his ideas on the nature of power and authority continue to influence discussions about leadership and governance. Amusingly, the English thinker Bertrand Russel, called it a manual for mobs.

Yet, despite its importance, the concept of human dignity remains elusive and difficult to define. It is a term that can mean different things to different people, and its application can be fraught with challenges and limitations. This book seeks to unpack the meaning and significance of human dignity, exploring its philosophical foundations, its role in social justice movements, and its practical applications in healthcare, criminal justice, and social policy.

THERE ARE MANY REASONS
WHY SOMEONE MIGHT WRITE
A BOOK ON DIGNITY

Here are a few possible reasons:

• To explore the philosophical and moral dimensions of the concept of dignity, and to examine how it has been understood and interpreted throughout history.

• To investigate how dignity is related to human rights, social justice, and equality, and to explore how it can be used to promote greater fairness and respect in society.

• To examine the ways in which dignity can be threatened or violated in various contexts, such as in the workplace, in relationships, or in political systems.

• To offer guidance and strategies for cultivating and maintaining dignity in one's own life, and for promoting dignity in others.

• To contribute to ongoing debates and discussions about the importance and relevance of dignity in contemporary society, and to advocate for its recognition and protection.

But I beg the reader not to rely too much on history; reasoning by analogy is too common and fallacious, often a trap.

IS THERE ANY SYMBOLISM?

There is no specific symbol associated with the concept of dignity. However, throughout history, different cultures have used various symbols to represent dignity or aspects of it. For example, in Ancient Greek culture, the owl was seen as a symbol of wisdom, which is closely related to dignity. In Hinduism, the lotus flower is a symbol of purity, enlightenment, and spiritual growth, which are all related to the concept of dignity. Additionally, some religious traditions use particular colors or items to represent dignity or related concepts. For instance, in Christianity, the color purple is often associated with dignity, as it was historically used to represent royalty and nobility.

The recognition and protection of human dignity is the foundation of human rights, and its violation is at the root of many of the world's most pressing social problems. We all have a responsibility to protect and promote human dignity, both in our personal interactions and in our larger social and political systems. Only by recognizing the inherent worth and value of every human being can we create a world that is just, equitable, and compassionate.

DEFINITION OF DIGNITY AND ITS IMPORTANCE

In this section, we'll start by defining what we mean by "dignity". Dignity is a complex and multifaceted concept, but at its core, it is often understood to refer to a person's inherent worth and value as a human being. This worth is not dependent on any particular trait or characteristic, such as intelligence, wealth, or social status, but is seen as an intrinsic quality that is shared by all human beings simply by virtue of their humanity.

Dignity is often associated with notions of respect, honor, and self-esteem. It is seen as a fundamental aspect of human identity and relationships, and is closely linked to ideas of autonomy, agency, and self-determination. The concept of dignity is also frequently invoked in discussions of human rights, social justice, and ethical decision-making.

The importance of the concept of dignity can be seen in its wide-ranging implications for various aspects of human life. For example, in healthcare, dignity is often seen as a critical component of high-quality care, and is associated with respectful and compassionate treatment of patients. In the workplace, dignity can be a key factor in promoting a positive and inclusive work environment, and in promoting employees' sense of self-worth and self-respect. In the realm of politics and social justice, dignity is often invoked as a basis for demanding equal treatment and rights for all individuals, regardless of their background or status.

Overall, the concept of dignity plays a crucial role in shaping our understanding of what it means to be human, and in guiding our interactions with others. In the rest of the book, we will explore some of the key debates and issues surrounding the concept of dignity, and examine its implications for various aspects of human life and society.

BRIEF HISTORY OF THE
CONCEPT OF DIGNITY

The concept of dignity has a long and complex history, and has been understood and valued in different ways by different cultures and societies throughout time. In ancient Greece, for example, the concept of dignity was closely tied to ideas of honor and reputation, and was associated with the status and social standing of individuals within their community. In ancient Rome, the concept of dignity was similarly linked to ideas of social rank and status, and was often associated with the dignitas, or social prestige, of an individual or family.

During the Middle Ages, the concept of dignity took on new religious and philosophical significance, particularly in the context of Christian theology. In the work of theologians such as Thomas Aquinas, dignity was understood as a fundamental aspect of human nature, rooted in the belief that all human beings were created in the image of God. This understanding of dignity as an intrinsic quality of human beings would go on to shape subsequent philosophical and political debates about the rights and worth of individuals.

During the Enlightenment period, the concept of dignity underwent further evolution and development, particularly in the work of thinkers such as Immanuel Kant. For Kant, dignity was understood as a fundamental aspect of human autonomy and freedom, and was closely linked to the concept of human rights. Kant's work would go on to influence subsequent debates about the value and importance of dignity in ethics, law, and politics.

In more recent times, the concept of dignity has continued to play an important role in various aspects of human life and society. The development of international human rights law, for example, has been based in large part on the idea that all human beings possess an inherent dignity that must be respected and protected. In the field of healthcare, dignity has become an increasingly important consideration in the treatment of patients, with many healthcare providers emphasizing the importance of providing care that is respectful, compassionate, and promotes patients' sense of dignity and self-worth.

Overall, the concept of dignity has a rich and complex history, shaped by various philosophical, religious, and cultural traditions. Understanding this history is important for gaining a deeper appreciation of the importance of dignity as a concept in contemporary society, and for exploring its ongoing implications for various aspects of human life and relationships.

THE IMPORTANCE TO BE HUMAN

Throughout the history of humankind, dignity has been a fundamental lesson that men have evolved with. It has been recognized as an essential element of what it means to be human, and has been an integral part of many cultures and traditions. In ancient times, for example, the concept of honor was closely linked to dignity. Honor was not just about reputation or prestige, but about the intrinsic value of a person. It was about living up to a set of ethical standards that recognized the worth and dignity of all people, regardless of their status or position in society.

Similarly, many religions and spiritual traditions have emphasized the importance of treating others with dignity and respect. From the Golden Rule in Christianity to the concept of Ahimsa in Hinduism and Buddhism, the message is clear: treat others as you would like to be treated, and recognize the inherent worth and dignity of all beings.

In more recent times, the concept of human rights has become a central theme in the struggle for dignity and justice. The Universal Declaration of Human Rights, adopted by the United Nations in 1948, recognized the inherent dignity and worth of all human beings, and set forth a framework for protecting and promoting those rights.

Overall, the lesson of dignity has been an important one throughout human history, reminding us that every person has value and worth, and deserves to be treated with respect and compassion. It is a lesson that continues to be relevant today, as we face new challenges and struggles in the quest for a more just and compassionate world.

Early cultures placed a great emphasis on dignity as a fundamental value. In many tribal societies, for example, dignity was tied to the idea of respect for elders and the wisdom that comes with age. In many Native American cultures, for instance, the concept of respect was central to the idea of dignity. Respect was shown not only to elders, but also to nature and the environment, and to the traditions and customs of the tribe. In ancient civilizations like Egypt and China, dignity was linked to the concept of justice. Leaders were expected to uphold the principles of fairness and equality, and to treat their subjects with respect and dignity. Similarly, in Greece, the concept of dignity was linked to the idea of honor, which was seen as a core value of the culture.

Throughout history, various forms of art and literature have also emphasized the importance of dignity. For example, Shakespeare's plays often explored themes of honor and dignity, and depicted characters who struggled to maintain their dignity in difficult circumstances. In the visual arts, many works of art depict individuals with a strong sense of dignity, even in the face of adversity.

IN THE EYES OF THE MAESTRO

In the masterpiece "The Last Supper" by Leonardo da Vinci, the concept of dignity can also be interpreted through the lens of the American philosopher and psychologist William James. James believed that dignity was closely linked to the concept of self-esteem, or the degree to which individuals value and respect themselves. In "The Last Supper," we see a depiction of the final meal that Jesus shared with his disciples before his crucifixion, and this scene can be seen as a powerful example of how individuals can maintain their dignity even in the face of adversity.

Despite the impending betrayal and execution of Jesus, the figures in the painting are shown with a sense of calm and composure that reflects their inner strength and self-assurance. James might argue that this sense of dignity arises from the fact that each individual in the painting has a strong sense of self-esteem and a clear understanding of their own value and worth as human beings. Furthermore, James believed that individuals could cultivate their sense of dignity and self-esteem through a process of self-reflection and self-awareness. By taking the time to reflect on their own values and beliefs, individuals can develop a sense of inner strength and confidence that allows them to maintain their dignity even in difficult circumstances.

For Hegel, dignity is a fundamental aspect of human consciousness and self-awareness, and is linked to our ability to recognize and respect the dignity of others. In "The Last Supper," we see a depiction of the final meal that Jesus shared with his disciples before his crucifixion. The painting captures the moment when Jesus announces that one of his disciples will betray him, causing a moment of tension and despair among the group.

Despite this betrayal, however, the painting also portrays a sense of dignity and nobility among the figures in the scene. Jesus himself is depicted as calm and composed, with a sense of gravitas and authority that conveys his status as a spiritual leader. The other figures are also shown with a sense of dignity and humanity, even as they struggle with their own doubts and fears.

Hegel might argue that this sense of dignity arises from the fact that each individual in the painting is recognized and valued for their unique identity and consciousness. In Hegelian terms, the figures in the painting are seen as "self-determining" beings, capable of making their own choices and decisions in life. By recognizing and respecting this dignity in others, we are able to build meaningful relationships and create a just and compassionate society.

Overall, "The Last Supper" can be seen as a powerful representation of the concept of dignity, both in terms of its depiction of Jesus and the other figures in the scene. Through its portrayal of the complexity and nuance of human relationships, the painting speaks to the importance of recognizing and respecting the inherent worth and value of every individual. My final observation, after reading Da Vinci's journals and his theory of 'Saper Vedere' (ability to see), taught me that every detail has a purpose, including the shadows.

UNDERSTANDING DIGNITY

There are different philosophical frameworks for understanding dignity, and two of the most prominent are deontological and consequentialist approaches.

Deontological approaches to dignity focus on the inherent value and rights of individuals, regardless of the consequences of our actions. This means that individuals are treated as ends in themselves, rather than as means to an end. In this framework, dignity is seen as an absolute and universal principle that must be respected at all times, regardless of the consequences. Immanuel Kant's ethical theory is an example of a deontological approach to dignity, where he believed that all human beings have inherent worth and dignity, and that we must treat them as such, regardless of the consequences. More on the next section.

Consequentialist approaches to dignity, on the other hand, focus on the consequences of our actions and the overall well-being of individuals and society. In this framework, dignity is seen as a relative principle that can be outweighed by other values, such as the promotion of well-being. Utilitarianism is an example of a consequentialist approach to dignity, where the moral value of an action is determined by the amount of overall well-being it produces.

Both deontological and consequentialist approaches have strengths and weaknesses when it comes to understanding dignity. Deontological approaches provide a strong foundation for respecting the inherent value and rights of individuals, but can be rigid and inflexible in certain situations. Consequentialist approaches are more flexible and adaptable, but can be criticized for potentially violating the dignity and rights of individuals in the pursuit of overall well-being.

Ultimately, the philosophical framework we use to understand dignity will depend on our ethical and moral beliefs, as well as the specific situation and context in which we find ourselves.

A BRIEF OVERVIEW OF HOW PHILOSOPHERS HAVE CONTRIBUTED TO THE DEVELOPMENT OF THE CONCEPT OF DIGNITY

Immanuel Kant: Kant is perhaps best known for his moral philosophy, which emphasizes the importance of reason and autonomy. In his work, he argued that human beings have an inherent dignity that must be respected, and that this dignity is based on our capacity for rational thought and moral decision-making. According to Kant, each individual has a duty to respect the dignity of others, as previously discussed.

Kant believed that human beings have an inherent worth and dignity that must be respected, and that this dignity is based on our capacity for rational thought and moral decision-making. Kant's idea of the categorical imperative is central to his moral philosophy, and is closely linked to the concept of dignity. The categorical imperative is a moral principle that requires us to treat other people as ends in themselves, rather than as means to an end. In other words, we should always treat others with dignity and respect, and not use them for our own purposes. Kant also believed that dignity is closely linked to the concept of autonomy, or the ability to make our own decisions and act on our own values and beliefs. For Kant, autonomy is a central part of our dignity as human beings, and we must work to cultivate and protect it throughout our lives.

Overall, Kant's ideas about dignity have had a profound impact on our understanding of the value and importance of each individual, and on our moral obligations to treat others with respect and empathy.

Aristotle: Aristotle was a Greek philosopher who lived in the 4th century BCE. He believed that human beings have a natural capacity for rational thought and moral decision-making, and that this capacity is what sets us apart from other animals. For Aristotle, dignity is closely linked to our capacity for reason, and it is something that we must work to develop and cultivate throughout our lives.

He is widely regarded as one of the most important figures in Western philosophy. He contributed to a wide range of fields, including ethics, politics, metaphysics, and biology.

In terms of the concept of dignity, Aristotle believed that human beings have a natural capacity for rational thought and moral decision-making, which is what sets us apart from other animals. He believed that this capacity for reason is what gives us our dignity as human beings, and that it is something that we must work to develop and cultivate throughout our lives.

For Aristotle, dignity is closely linked to the idea of eudaimonia, or human flourishing. He believed that human beings have an innate desire to live a good life, and that this can only be achieved through the cultivation of virtue and the pursuit of excellence. According to Aristotle, we can only achieve eudaimonia by living in accordance with our rational nature, and by cultivating the virtues that allow us to do so.

Aristotle believed that the virtues were essential for living a good life, and that they were closely linked to the concept of dignity. He believed that the virtues were a way of living in accordance with our rational nature, and that they allowed us to achieve excellence in all aspects of our lives. He believed that the virtues were essential for promoting human flourishing, and that they were necessary for creating a just and harmonious society.

Overall, Aristotle's ideas about dignity have had a profound impact on our understanding of what it means to be human, and on our moral obligations to cultivate and protect our rational nature. His ideas about eudaimonia and the virtues continue to be influential today, and are central to many discussions about the nature of human flourishing and the good life.

Georg Wilhelm Friedrich Hegel: Hegel was a German philosopher who lived in the 19th century. He is known for his work on dialectics, which is a method of reasoning that involves the synthesis of opposing viewpoints. In his work, Hegel argued that human beings have an inherent dignity that is based on our capacity for rational thought and our ability to recognize and appreciate the dignity of others. He believed that this recognition of dignity is essential for creating harmonious and just societies, and that it is something that we must work to cultivate through our interactions with others.

Hegel is widely regarded as one of the most influential figures in the history of philosophy. He made significant contributions to a wide range of fields, including epistemology, metaphysics, ethics, and political theory.

In terms of the concept of dignity, Hegel believed that it was closely linked to the idea of freedom, and that it was essential for creating a just and harmonious society. He believed that human beings have an inherent dignity that must be respected, and that this dignity is based on our capacity for self-determination and moral decision-making.

Hegel believed that human beings have an innate desire for freedom, and that this desire is what gives us our dignity as human beings. He argued that each individual has a duty to respect the dignity of others, and to work towards creating a society that is based on freedom, justice, and equality.

Hegel's ideas about dignity and freedom were closely linked to his political philosophy, which emphasized the importance of the state in promoting the common good. He believed that the state had a duty to protect the dignity and freedom of its citizens, and that it was responsible for creating a society that was based on justice and equality.

In particular, Hegel's ideas about dignity and freedom have had a significant impact on our understanding of the nature of human beings, and on our moral and political obligations to promote human flourishing and social justice. His ideas continue to be influential today, and are often cited in discussions about the role of the state in promoting the common good, and the importance of human dignity in ethical and political decision-making.

These philosophers, along with many others, have contributed to the development of the concept of dignity over the centuries. Their work has helped to shape our understanding of what dignity is, why it is important, and how it can be promoted and protected in different contexts.

THE RELATIONSHIP BETWEEN DIGNITY AND HUMAN RIGHTS.

Dignity and human rights are closely linked concepts. Human rights are a set of entitlements that individuals possess simply by virtue of being human. These rights are intended to protect the inherent dignity of each individual and promote their well-being, freedom, and equality.

The Universal Declaration of Human Rights, adopted by the United Nations General Assembly in 1948, as previously mentioned, recognized the inherent dignity and worth of every human being as the foundation of freedom, justice, and peace in the world. The declaration includes a range of rights, such as the right to life, liberty, and security of person, the right to freedom of thought, conscience, and religion, and the right to education, work, and social security.

The idea that human beings possess inherent dignity and rights is also reflected in many national constitutions and legal systems. For example, the United States Constitution includes the Bill of Rights, which protects individual rights such as freedom of speech, religion, and assembly. Similarly, the European Convention on Human Rights protects a range of civil, political, and social rights, including the right to a fair trial, freedom from torture and inhuman or degrading treatment, and the right to respect for private and family life.

Dignity and human rights are often seen as mutually reinforcing concepts. The protection of human rights is necessary to respect the inherent dignity of each individual, while the recognition of inherent dignity is the foundation for the protection of human rights. Both concepts are essential for promoting the well-being, freedom, and equality of individuals and for creating a just and peaceful society.

However, there are also challenges and tensions. For example, there may be situations where the protection of individual rights conflicts with the well-being and safety of society as a whole. In these cases, it may be necessary to balance individual rights with the greater good of society, while still respecting the inherent dignity of each individual.

EXAMINATION OF THE ROLE OF DIGNITY IN INTERNATIONAL HUMAN RIGHTS LAW

International human rights law plays a significant role in promoting and protecting the dignity of every individual. The idea that human beings possess inherent dignity and rights is enshrined in various international human rights instruments and treaties. Here are some examples:

Universal Declaration of Human Rights (UDHR): The UDHR, adopted by the United Nations General Assembly in 1948, recognizes the inherent dignity and worth of every human being and identifies a range of human rights that should be protected to promote individual freedom, justice, and peace in the world. The UDHR has been translated into more than 500 languages and is widely recognized as a foundational document of international human rights law.

International Covenant on Civil and Political Rights (ICCPR): The ICCPR is a treaty adopted by the United Nations General Assembly in 1966. It recognizes a range of civil and political rights, including the right to life, freedom of expression, and freedom of thought, conscience, and religion. The ICCPR also includes provisions that protect the inherent dignity of individuals, such as the prohibition of torture, cruel, inhuman or degrading treatment or punishment, and the right to be treated with humanity and respect for the inherent dignity of the human person.

International Covenant on Economic, Social, and Cultural Rights (ICESCR): The ICESCR is another treaty adopted by the United Nations General Assembly in 1966. It recognizes a range of economic, social, and cultural rights, such as the right to work, education, and healthcare. The ICESCR also includes provisions that recognize the importance of human dignity, such as the right to an adequate standard of living and the right to enjoy the benefits of scientific progress and its applications.

Convention on the Rights of the Child (CRC): The CRC is a treaty adopted by the United Nations General Assembly in 1989. It recognizes the inherent dignity of children and identifies a range of rights that should be protected to promote their well-being, development, and protection. The CRC recognizes the right of every child to a standard of living adequate for their physical, mental, spiritual, moral, and social development, and the right to participate fully in cultural and social life.

These instruments and treaties, sometime undervalued, highlight the importance of dignity in international human rights law. The recognition of inherent dignity and the protection of human rights are essential for promoting the well-being, freedom, and equality of individuals and for creating a just and peaceful society.

DISCUSSION OF THE WAYS IN WHICH HUMAN RIGHTS VIOLATIONS CAN CONSTITUTE AN ATTACK ON HUMAN DIGNITY

Human rights violations can constitute an attack on human dignity because they can harm or undermine the fundamental aspects of a person's life that contribute to their inherent worth and value as a human being. Here are some examples of how human rights violations can constitute an attack on human dignity:

Denial of basic needs: When people are denied access to basic needs such as food, water, shelter, and healthcare, their physical and mental health can suffer, and their dignity can be undermined. People who are unable to meet their basic needs may feel helpless, vulnerable, and powerless, which can erode their sense of self-worth and dignity.

Discrimination: Discrimination on the basis of race, gender, sexual orientation, religion, or any other personal characteristic can be dehumanizing and can undermine a person's sense of dignity. Discrimination can limit a person's opportunities, exclude them from participating fully in society, and stigmatize them, leading to feelings of shame and inferiority.

Torture and cruel treatment: Torture and other forms of cruel, inhuman, or degrading treatment can be deeply traumatic and violate a person's bodily integrity and autonomy. These practices can inflict physical and psychological pain and suffering, and can cause lasting harm to a person's sense of self-worth and dignity.

Forced labor and exploitation: When people are forced to work without fair compensation or under conditions of exploitation, their labor is devalued, and their sense of self-worth and dignity can be undermined. Forced labor can also limit a person's opportunities and autonomy, leading to feelings of powerlessness and vulnerability.

Violations of privacy and personal autonomy: When people's privacy and personal autonomy are violated, their sense of control over their lives can be eroded, and their dignity can be undermined. For example, surveillance, censorship, and arbitrary detention can limit a person's freedom of expression and movement, leading to feelings of isolation and helplessness.

In summary, human rights violations can constitute an attack on human dignity by harming or undermining the fundamental aspects of a person's life that contribute to their inherent worth and value as a human being. The protection of human rights is essential for promoting dignity, equality, and justice for all.

OVERVIEW OF THE HISTORICAL AND CONTEMPORARY SOCIAL JUSTICE MOVEMENTS THAT HAVE INVOKED THE CONCEPT OF DIGNITY

Civil Rights Movement: The Civil Rights Movement in the United States during the 1950s and 1960s invoked the concept of dignity in its struggle for racial equality. Leaders such as Martin Luther King Jr. argued that every individual, regardless of their race or ethnicity, possessed inherent dignity and worth, and that segregation and discrimination were violations of this dignity.

The Civil Rights Movement in the United States was one of the most significant social justice movements of the 20th century. It was a movement aimed at ending racial segregation and discrimination against African Americans, and promoting their civil and political rights.

The movement used a variety of tactics to achieve its goals, including nonviolent protests, civil disobedience, and legal challenges. Some of the most famous events in the Civil Rights Movement include the Montgomery Bus Boycott, the March on Washington, and the Selma to Montgomery March.

The Civil Rights Act of 1964, which outlawed discrimination based on race, color, religion, sex, or national origin, was a major victory for the Civil Rights Movement. However, the struggle for racial equality and the protection of human dignity continues to this day, as systemic racism and discrimination continue to affect many communities in the United States.

LGBTQ+ Rights Movement: The fight for LGBTQ+ rights has been centered on the recognition of the inherent dignity and worth of individuals who identify as lesbian, gay, bisexual, transgender, or queer. Advocates have argued that denying individuals the right to marry, access healthcare, or participate in public life based on their sexual orientation or gender identity is a violation of their dignity.

The LGBTQ+ rights movement has been a powerful force in promoting the recognition of dignity for all individuals, regardless of sexual orientation or gender identity. At its core, the movement has sought to challenge the notion that there is something inherently wrong or shameful about being LGBTQ+, and to assert the right of all individuals to live with dignity and respect.

Throughout history, LGBTQ+ individuals have faced discrimination and persecution in many different forms, including legal and social discrimination, violence, and hate crimes. In many countries, same-sex relationships were criminalized and LGBTQ+ individuals were subject to imprisonment, torture, and even death. The LGBTQ+ rights movement has fought against these injustices, working to secure legal protections for LGBTQ+ individuals and to promote greater social acceptance and understanding.

One of the key ways in which the LGBTQ+ rights movement has promoted dignity is by challenging the idea that heterosexuality and traditional gender roles are the only legitimate ways of being. The movement has sought to expand the definition of what it means to be human, and to affirm the diversity of human experience. By doing so, it has helped to promote greater tolerance and understanding of differences, and to promote the dignity of all individuals.

The movement has also worked to secure legal protections for LGBTQ+ individuals, including the right to marry and the right to be protected from discrimination in employment, housing, and public accommodations. These legal protections have helped to promote the recognition of the dignity of LGBTQ+ individuals, and to ensure that they are treated with respect and equality under the law.

Overall, it has been a powerful force in promoting the

recognition of dignity for all individuals, and in challenging the unjust and discriminatory treatment of LGBTQ+ individuals throughout history. Through its work, the movement has helped to promote greater understanding, tolerance, and acceptance of all individuals, regardless of sexual orientation or gender identity.

Disability Rights Movement: The disability rights movement has invoked the concept of dignity in its struggle for equal rights and opportunities for people with disabilities. Advocates have argued that individuals with disabilities possess inherent dignity and worth, and that policies and practices that deny them access to education, employment, and community participation are violations of this dignity.

The disability rights movement emerged in the mid-twentieth century and aimed to improve the rights and living conditions of people with disabilities. Prior to this movement, people with disabilities were often marginalized and excluded from many aspects of society, such as education and employment.

The movement emphasized the dignity and worth of all individuals, regardless of their physical or mental abilities. It also called for the removal of physical and attitudinal barriers that prevented people with disabilities from fully participating in society.

One of the key figures in the disability rights movement was Ed Roberts, who contracted polio as a child and was paralyzed from the neck down. Roberts became an activist for disability rights and helped to establish the first Center for Independent Living in Berkeley, California in 1972.

The disability rights movement achieved a number of important victories, such as the passage of the Americans with Disabilities Act (ADA) in 1990. The ADA prohibits discrimination against people with disabilities in employment, transportation, public accommodations, and telecommunications.

The disability rights movement continues to advocate for the full inclusion and participation of people with disabilities in all aspects of society. This includes promoting accessible housing, transportation, and education, as well as challenging negative attitudes and stereotypes about people with disabilities.

Feminist Movement: The feminist movement has invoked the concept of dignity in its struggle for gender equality. Feminists have argued that women possess inherent dignity and worth, and that policies and practices that deny them equal rights and opportunities based on their gender are violations of this dignity.

The feminist movement emerged in the late 19th and early 20th centuries and aimed to achieve gender equality and women's rights. The movement emphasized the dignity and worth of women and called for an end to discrimination and oppression based on gender.

One of the key figures in the feminist movement was suffragist leader Susan B. Anthony, who fought for women's right to vote in the United States. Other important figures in the feminist movement include Betty Friedan, who wrote the influential book "The Feminine Mystique" in 1963, and Gloria Steinem, who co-founded Ms. Magazine in 1972.

The movement achieved a number of important victories, such as the passage of the 19th Amendment to the U.S. Constitution in 1920, which granted women the right to vote. The movement also helped to secure equal rights for women in education, employment, and other areas.

It continues to advocate for gender equality and the protection of women's rights. This includes fighting for equal pay, reproductive rights, and an end to gender-based violence and harassment. The movement also seeks to challenge patriarchal norms and stereotypes that contribute to the marginalization and oppression of women.

MeToo movement: The MeToo movement is a global movement that has emerged in response to the widespread prevalence of sexual harassment and assault, particularly in the workplace. The movement began in 2006, but gained widespread attention in 2017 when allegations of sexual misconduct were made against several high-profile figures in the entertainment industry. Since then, the movement has continued to grow and has inspired many individuals to speak out about their own experiences.

It is important to acknowledge that the MeToo movement has helped to raise awareness of the issue, and has encouraged many people to come forward with their stories, but there's a wrinkle: a torrent of false accusations.

While there may be many cases where false accusations have been made, it is important to remember that the vast majority of claims are made in good faith, and that the experiences of survivors of sex predators are valid and deserve to be heard.

Furthermore, the MeToo movement has helped to bring about important changes in the way that misconduct cases are addressed, including changes in workplace policies and legal protections for survivors.

It is certainly important to approach all claims with a critical eye and to evaluate them based on the available evidence. Skepticism can be a healthy and necessary part of any discussion, particularly when it comes to sensitive and complex issues such as sexual torment.

However, it is also important to recognize that skepticism should not be used as a tool to dismiss or invalidate the experiences of survivors. While false accusations do occur, the vast majority of individuals who come forward with their stories do so in good faith and have experienced significant trauma as a result of their experiences.

It is also important to recognize that skepticism can sometimes be used to perpetuate harmful myths and stereotypes about sexual harassment. For example, the idea that victims should immediately report their experiences to law enforcement or face accusations of lying is often used to discourage individuals from coming forward with their stories.

Instead of focusing solely on skepticism, it is important to approach the issue of sexual harassment and assault with empathy, understanding, and a willingness to listen to and support survivors. This means creating safe spaces where survivors can come forward with their stories, ensuring that all allegations are taken seriously and investigated thoroughly, and working towards creating a culture that is more respectful and equitable for all individuals.

Movement for Refugee Rights: The movement for refugee rights has invoked the concept of dignity in its struggle for the recognition and protection of the rights of refugees and asylum seekers. Advocates have argued that refugees possess inherent dignity and worth, and that policies and practices that deny them access to protection, healthcare, and other basic needs are violations of this dignity.

The movement for refugee rights seeks to protect the dignity and human rights of refugees who have been forced to flee their homes due to conflict, persecution, or other forms of violence. Refugees face a number of challenges, including discrimination, marginalization, and inadequate access to basic necessities such as food, shelter, and healthcare.

One of the key organizations in the movement for refugee rights is the United Nations High Commissioner for Refugees (UNHCR), which works to protect refugees and advocate for their rights. The UNHCR provides assistance and support to refugees in a number of ways, such as by providing shelter, food, and medical care.

In addition to the UNHCR, there are a number of grassroots organizations and advocacy groups working to protect the rights of refugees. These groups work to raise awareness about the challenges facing refugees, advocate for policy changes that support refugee rights, and provide direct support to refugees in need.

The movement for refugee rights also emphasizes the importance of addressing the root causes of displacement, such as conflict and inequality. By addressing these underlying issues, the movement seeks to prevent further displacement and protect the dignity and human rights of all people, including refugees.

These are just a few examples of the many social justice movements that have invoked the concept of dignity in their struggles for justice and equality.

SOCIAL INJUSTICE AND ITS IMPACT ON DIGNITY: THE NEED FOR A CULTURE OF EQUITY AND INCLUSION

Social injustices can undermine human dignity in a multitude of ways. For example, discrimination based on race, gender, sexuality, religion, or disability can lead to exclusion, marginalization, and the denial of basic human rights. This can cause individuals and communities to experience a sense of worthlessness, powerlessness, and degradation. Economic inequality can also undermine dignity by limiting access to education, healthcare, housing, and other basic needs. Lack of access to these necessities can lead to a sense of shame and humiliation, which can be detrimental to a person's sense of dignity. Additionally, systemic issues such as police brutality, mass incarceration, and the criminalization of poverty can also violate human dignity by perpetuating cycles of harm and trauma.

Furthermore, environmental degradation, climate change, and other global crises can also undermine human dignity by threatening basic living conditions, health, and safety. For example, the impacts of climate change disproportionately affect marginalized communities, exacerbating existing social and economic inequalities. The loss of biodiversity and destruction of ecosystems also threaten the well-being and dignity of non-human animals and the natural world.

In order to promote social justice and protect human dignity, it is important to address these underlying structural issues and work towards a more equitable and sustainable society. This requires a commitment to upholding the human rights of all individuals, regardless of their background or status. It also involves challenging systemic inequalities and working towards creating more just and inclusive social, economic, and political systems. Ultimately, promoting human dignity is not only a moral imperative, but also crucial for building a more peaceful and sustainable world for all.

In order to address the systemic issues that undermine human dignity, it is important to acknowledge the historical and ongoing injustices that have contributed to these problems. This involves examining how power and privilege operate within society and working towards dismantling the structures that perpetuate inequality.

One approach to promoting social justice and human dignity is through intersectional analysis, which recognizes that different forms of oppression are interconnected and intersecting. This approach emphasizes the need to address the multiple forms of marginalization that individuals may experience based on their race, gender, sexuality, disability, and other factors.

Another important strategy is community-based organizing, which involves bringing together individuals and groups who are affected by social injustices and working towards collective action and change. This approach emphasizes the importance of empowering communities to be agents of change, and recognizes the role of grassroots movements in promoting social justice and human dignity.

Overall, promoting human dignity requires a commitment to addressing systemic inequalities, challenging structures of power and privilege, and working towards creating a more just and inclusive society. By centering human dignity in our actions and policies, we can work towards a world that upholds the inherent worth and value of all individuals, regardless of their background or status.

POLICE ABUSE AND ITS IMPACT ON SOCIETY: THE EROSION OF TRUST AND THE NEED FOR ACCOUNTABILITY

Police abuse is a serious problem that can have far-reaching consequences for individuals and society as a whole. When police officers abuse their power and engage in unlawful or unethical behavior, it can erode public trust in law enforcement and undermine the rule of law.

In a police state, the government exercises an excessive degree of control over its citizens, often using the police to enforce its will. This type of government is often seen as oppressive and authoritarian, and it can lead to widespread human rights abuses, including police brutality and the violation of civil liberties.

From the perspective of the international community, a police state is embarrassing and concerning. Countries that are known to have a history of police abuse may face diplomatic isolation or economic sanctions, as other nations seek to distance themselves from these human rights violations.

Moreover, a police state can also negatively impact the daily lives of citizens, as they may feel like they are constantly being monitored and controlled by the police. This can lead to a sense of fear and mistrust, making it difficult for people to go about their daily lives freely and without fear of harassment or violence.

To prevent police abuse and the development of a police state, it is important to have strong oversight mechanisms in place to ensure that law enforcement officials are held accountable for their actions. This can involve independent investigations of alleged police misconduct, increased training for officers, and the establishment of civilian review boards to oversee police activities.

Additionally, it is important to create a culture of respect for human rights and the rule of law, both within law enforcement agencies and society as a whole. This can involve education campaigns to raise awareness about the importance of civil liberties and to promote a culture of nonviolence and respect for human dignity.

In conclusion, police abuse and the development of a police state are serious issues that can have far-reaching consequences for individuals and society as a whole. By working together to prevent police abuse and promote respect for human rights, we can create a safer, more just, and more equitable world for everyone.

THE DAMAGING EFFECTS OF DEGRADING STUDENTS: THE ROLE OF FLAWED TEACHING METHODS IN UNDERPERFORMANCE

This is a very bad one. The education system plays a critical role in shaping the future of society by equipping students with the knowledge and skills they need to succeed in life. However, when teachers degrade and belittle students who are underperforming, they can do serious damage to their self-esteem and confidence, which can have long-lasting effects.

When students are young and vulnerable, they are not fully equipped to understand and respond to negative feedback in the same way as adults. If a teacher consistently degrades and humiliates a student who is struggling, it can lead to feelings of shame, worthlessness, and inadequacy. These feelings can be internalized and can affect the student's motivation to learn, leading to a cycle of underperformance and negative feedback.

Furthermore, when teachers blame students for underperforming rather than recognizing flaws in the teaching methods or curriculum, it perpetuates an unfair system that places the burden of responsibility solely on the student. In reality, the teaching methods and curriculum are just as responsible for student outcomes as the students themselves. Therefore, it is essential for teachers to take a critical look at their teaching methods and curriculum and make necessary changes to help students succeed.

It is also important to recognize that students come from diverse backgrounds and may face different challenges that affect their academic performance. Rather than degrading students who are struggling, teachers should strive to create a supportive and inclusive learning environment that recognizes and accommodates the unique needs of each student.

RESPECT YOUR ELDERS: A LOOK AT THE HISTORICAL SIGNIFICANCE OF HONORING SENIOR CITIZENS AND UPHOLDING DIGNITY IN SOCIETY

Throughout history, elders have been respected and venerated in many societies. In many traditional cultures, elders were considered to be wise and knowledgeable, and their opinions and advice were highly valued. They often served as leaders and decision-makers in their communities, and their experience and expertise were considered to be essential to the well-being of their societies.

For example, in many Indigenous cultures around the world, elders are revered and respected as sources of wisdom and guidance. They are often considered to be the keepers of traditional knowledge and are responsible for passing on cultural traditions and teachings to younger generations.

Similarly, in many Asian cultures, elders are highly respected and venerated. Confucianism, a philosophy that originated in China over 2,000 years ago, emphasizes the importance of filial piety and respect for elders. This includes showing deference to one's parents, grandparents, and other elders, and honoring their wisdom and experience.

Even in Western cultures, where youth and innovation are often emphasized, elders have played important roles throughout history. For example, in ancient Greece, the elders were highly respected and often served as advisors to the rulers of the city-states. In medieval Europe, the elderly were often valued for their knowledge and experience, and they were often consulted on matters of governance and policy.

Overall, throughout history and across cultures, elders have been respected and valued for their wisdom, experience, and contributions to society. It is important that we continue to recognize and honor the dignity of our elders in modern society as well. However, there's a horrific trend on the horizon.

Elder abuse is a serious issue that affects millions of seniors around the world. This form of mistreatment can take many different forms, from physical and emotional abuse to financial exploitation and neglect. However, the root of the problem often lies in a lack of respect and veneration for elders in society.

It is important to recognize that seniors have a wealth of knowledge and life experience that is deserving of our respect and admiration. They have lived through wars, economic crises, and social upheavals, and have a unique perspective on the world that can offer valuable insights and guidance to younger generations.

Moreover, elders also have a right to dignity and autonomy, and should be treated with the same level of respect and compassion that we would want for ourselves. This means listening to their opinions, preferences, and needs, and providing them with the support and resources they need to live fulfilling and dignified lives.

In practical terms, this can involve everything from advocating for stronger legal protections for seniors to promoting intergenerational programs that foster mutual respect and understanding. It can also involve taking a more active role in the lives of the seniors in our own families and communities, whether by spending time with them, helping with errands, or simply listening to their stories and experiences.

Ultimately, by recognizing and venerating the elders in our society, we can create a culture of respect and dignity that benefits everyone, regardless of age or background.

THE PRACTICAL APPLICATIONS OF DIGNITY: HOW IT SHAPES HEALTHCARE, CRIMINAL JUSTICE, AND SOCIAL POLICY

The concept of dignity has practical applications in a wide range of contexts, including healthcare, criminal justice, and social policy. Here are some examples of how dignity can be applied in these contexts:

Healthcare: In healthcare, the concept of dignity is often used to guide ethical decision-making and ensure that patients are treated with respect and compassion. This includes providing patients with the information they need to make informed decisions about their care, preserving their privacy and autonomy, and treating them with dignity and compassion at all times.

Criminal justice: In the criminal justice system, the concept of dignity can be applied to ensure that defendants are treated fairly and humanely. This includes protecting their legal rights, providing them with access to legal representation, and ensuring that they are not subject to cruel or inhuman treatment.

Social policy: In the realm of social policy, the concept of dignity can be used to guide efforts to address inequality and promote social justice. This includes ensuring that all people have access to the basic resources they need to live with dignity, such as food, shelter, and healthcare. It also involves creating policies that are designed to promote dignity, such as efforts to reduce discrimination and promote inclusivity.

CHALLENGES AND LIMITATIONS OF APPLYING THE CONCEPT OF DIGNITY IN PRACTICE:

Cultural differences: The concept of dignity can be interpreted and applied in different ways depending on cultural context, which can pose challenges in situations where there are cultural differences between individuals or groups.

Legal and policy frameworks: The practical application of the concept of dignity can be constrained by legal and policy frameworks, which may prioritize other values or goals over the protection and promotion of dignity.

Resource constraints: In situations where resources are limited, it can be difficult to prioritize the protection and promotion of dignity, which may be seen as a secondary concern compared to more basic needs such as food, shelter, and healthcare.

Power imbalances: In situations where there are power imbalances between individuals or groups, it can be difficult to protect and promote the dignity of those who are marginalized or disadvantaged.

Ethical dilemmas: In some situations, the protection and promotion of dignity may come into conflict with other ethical considerations, such as the need to protect public safety or to respect the autonomy of individuals.

By examining the challenges and limitations of applying the concept of dignity in practice, readers could gain a better understanding of the complexities involved in promoting human dignity, and of the need for careful consideration of the practical implications of the concept in different contexts. Overall, the concept of dignity has many practical applications in a variety of contexts. By applying the principles of dignity in these areas, we can work to ensure that all people are treated with respect, compassion, and fairness, and that their inherent worth and value as human beings are recognized and honored.

GOOD INTENTIONS AREN'T ENOUGH: WHY YOU NEED TO TRAIN FOR THE UNKNOWN AND TAKE CONTROL OF YOUR LIFE

While good intentions and ideas can be helpful, they may not always be enough to navigate the challenges and uncertainties of real-life situations. Therefore, it is important to invest in preparation and training to equip ourselves with the skills and knowledge needed to tackle the unknown.

This is particularly important in high-pressure environments, where quick thinking and decisive action can make all the difference. By taking the time to prepare and train, we can build the confidence and resilience needed to face unexpected challenges head-on. This can involve everything from practicing emergency drills to developing new skills or seeking out expert guidance and mentorship.

Ultimately, the key is to recognize that good intentions alone may not be enough to achieve our goals or overcome obstacles. By investing in our own development and taking proactive steps to prepare for the unexpected, we can better position ourselves for success and build a sense of personal agency and empowerment.

CHANCE AND THE BUSINESS OF LIFE

Many influential thinkers, including philosophers, scientists, and entrepreneurs, have recognized the role of chance or luck in the business of life. While some people may attribute success or failure solely to personal qualities such as hard work, intelligence, or talent, others acknowledge that external factors, such as luck or chance events, can also play a significant role.

One example of this is the concept of the "butterfly effect," which suggests that small changes or events can have a significant impact on larger systems or outcomes. In other words, even seemingly insignificant events can have far-reaching consequences.

Similarly, many successful entrepreneurs and businesspeople have acknowledged the role of luck in their success. While hard work and talent are certainly important, they recognize that external factors such as timing, market conditions, and even chance encounters can play a significant role in determining whether a business venture succeeds or fails.

Philosophers such as Aristotle and Seneca have also recognized the role of chance in human affairs. Aristotle, for example, believed that luck played a role in determining a person's fate, while Seneca wrote extensively about the importance of accepting the role of chance in life and developing the resilience to cope with unexpected events.

Moreover, many scientists and mathematicians have explored the role of chance and randomness in the natural world. The field of probability, for example, is based on the idea that many events are inherently uncertain and subject to chance.

THE FORTUNE COOKIE THAT LIED

What is the correlation with chance? Life is often a product of chance, as in game theory.

The fortune cookie analogy is a good example of the role of chance in our lives. Fortune cookies are often associated with luck and chance, as the fortunes inside are meant to provide a glimpse into the future or offer guidance or advice.

In the case of the fortune cookie, the message inside turned out to be incorrect or misleading. This underscores the inherent uncertainty and unpredictability of the future, and the role that chance or luck can play in shaping our lives.

Game theory is another area where chance and probability play a significant role. Game theory is the study of strategic decision-making in situations where the outcomes of one's choices depend on the choices of others. In such situations, chance and uncertainty can play a significant role in determining the optimal strategy.

For example, consider a game of poker. While skill and strategy are certainly important in winning at poker, chance also plays a significant role in determining the outcome of each hand. A skilled player may be able to maximize their chances of winning, but ultimately, the outcome of the game will depend in part on the cards that are dealt.

Similarly, in life, many outcomes are influenced by chance events or factors outside of our control. While we can certainly take steps to improve our chances of success or mitigate our risks, ultimately, chance will always play a role in determining the outcome.

In conclusion, the fortune cookie that lied and game theory are both examples of the role of chance in our lives. While we can certainly take steps to influence the outcome of events, chance and uncertainty will always be a part of the human experience. Acknowledging and accepting this reality can help us to approach life with greater humility, resilience, and openness to unexpected opportunities and challenges.

THE POWER OF DIGNITY AND HUMILITY: HOW SILENCE CAN DEMONSTRATE RESPECT AND SELF-CONTROL

First, dignity is often associated with a sense of self-respect and self-worth. When we act with dignity, we demonstrate a sense of confidence and composure, even in the face of difficult or challenging situations. At the same time, humility involves recognizing our limitations and shortcomings, and accepting that we are not perfect. By acknowledging our imperfections and limitations, we can approach others with a sense of humility and respect.

Silence, on the other hand, can be a powerful tool for demonstrating both dignity and humility. When we choose to remain silent rather than reacting impulsively or defensively, we can show a sense of self-control and restraint. This can be especially important in situations where our dignity or self-respect may be challenged. At the same time, silence can also be a form of humility, as it demonstrates a willingness to listen to others and to acknowledge their perspectives, even if they differ from our own.

Furthermore, silence can also be a way of demonstrating respect for others. When we choose to listen rather than speak, we can show a sense of humility and recognition of others' worth and value. This can be especially important in situations where there may be a power imbalance or where others may be vulnerable or marginalized.

Additionally, practicing humility and silence can also lead to greater self-awareness and personal growth. When we acknowledge our imperfections and limitations, we open ourselves up to the possibility of learning and improvement. By remaining silent and listening to others, we can gain valuable insights and perspectives that can help us to broaden our own understanding of the world around us.

Moreover, when we act with dignity, humility, and silence, we can also set an example for others to follow. By demonstrating these qualities in our own behavior, we can inspire others to do the same, creating a culture of respect, understanding, and compassion.

It's worth noting that there can be a fine line between silence and passivity. While remaining silent can be a powerful tool for demonstrating dignity and humility, there may be times when speaking up and taking action are necessary. In such situations, it's important to strike a balance between speaking out for what is right and demonstrating respect and consideration for others.

In conclusion, dignity, humility, and silence are interconnected qualities that can help us to build stronger, more respectful relationships with others and to cultivate personal growth and self-awareness. By striving to embody these qualities in our own behavior, we can create a more just and compassionate world, both for ourselves and for those around us.

FINAL THOUGHTS

In this book on dignity, we explored the concept's history and philosophical underpinnings, its role in human rights and social justice movements, and its practical applications in various contexts such as healthcare, criminal justice, and social policy. We discussed the challenges and limitations of applying the concept of dignity in practice, and examined how it can be protected and promoted in different situations.

Through our analysis, we found that dignity is a fundamental human value that is central to the promotion of social justice and human rights. It provides a framework for understanding the inherent worth and value of all individuals and communities, and offers a vision for a more just and equitable society.

We also explored the ways in which social injustices can undermine human dignity, and how the concept of dignity can be used to address structural inequalities and promote social change. In short, this book has shown that dignity is a powerful and transformative concept that can help us to create a more just and compassionate world.

As we reflect on the importance of dignity in contemporary society, it is clear that there is much work to be done in terms of research and activism. We must continue to explore the complexities of the concept of dignity and its implications for a wide range of issues, from healthcare to social justice movements. We must also consider the ways in which social injustices and structural inequalities can undermine human dignity and work towards addressing these issues.

Future research could focus on developing more nuanced understandings of dignity in different cultural and social contexts, as well as exploring the role of dignity in emerging fields such as AI and robotics. Activism could focus on promoting policies and practices that prioritize human dignity, such as increasing access to healthcare and education, addressing economic inequality, and promoting inclusive social policies.

Ultimately, the ongoing importance of dignity in contemporary society reminds us of the fundamental value of each and every human being. By continuing to prioritize dignity in our research and activism, we can work towards creating a more just and equitable world for all.

OPUS ES FACTO: THE POEM

I was thinking on finishing this short book with a food recipe, just to decompress, but, desperate in my search for a spaghetti sauce to 'dignify' my creation, I instead opted for a short bicycle trip on a mountain top in Southeast Asia and wrote a poem.

Standing atop this mountain peak,

I raise my voice for all to seek,
The essence of a noble trait,
That elevates us to a higher state.

Dignity, oh dignified grace,
In every human, finds its place,
The recognition of our inherent worth,
That deserves respect from the day of our birth.

It is the foundation of human rights,
And the pillar of social justice fights,
A call to treat every soul with equality,
And shun all forms of discrimination, in totality.

Let us embrace this virtue divine,
And let it guide us in every line,
To uplift the marginalized and oppressed,
And to create a world, that is just and blessed.

So let us pledge to uphold dignity,
As we climb down from this lofty spree,
And carry it with us in every action and thought,
To create a world, where every soul is sought.

TRACING THE EVOLUTION OF DIGNITY: A CHRONOLOGICAL JOURNEY THROUGH IMPORTANT HISTORICAL FACTS

• Ancient Greek philosopher Aristotle wrote extensively about dignity and its connection to moral virtues and ethics (4th century BCE).

• Roman statesman Cicero wrote about dignity as an inherent quality of human beings and the foundation of human rights (1st century BCE).

• The Judeo-Christian tradition emphasizes the importance of human dignity, with the creation of humans in the image of God serving as the basis for this belief (Old Testament, various authors and dates).

• In the Enlightenment era, Immanuel Kant developed a theory of dignity that emphasized the inherent worth of human beings, independent of their individual qualities or accomplishments (18th century CE).

• The Universal Declaration of Human Rights, adopted by the United Nations General Assembly in 1948, recognizes human dignity as the foundation of all human rights and freedoms.

• The civil rights movement of the 1950s and 60s in the United States was based on the belief that all human beings are entitled to equal dignity and respect, regardless of their race or ethnicity.

• The disability rights movement emerged in the 1960s and 70s, advocating for the recognition of the dignity and rights of people with disabilities.

• The feminist movement has emphasized the importance of recognizing the dignity of all individuals, regardless of their gender or sexuality.

• The concept of dignity continues to be an important part of international human rights law, and is frequently invoked in discussions of social justice and equality.

LIST OF KEYWORDS AND CONCEPTS

Human dignity
Philosophical foundations of dignity
Deontological and consequentialist approaches to dignity
Human rights and dignity
Social justice movements and dignity
LGBTQ+ rights movement and dignity
Disability rights movement and dignity
Feminist movement and dignity
Refugee rights movement and dignity
Promoting and protecting dignity
Social injustices and dignity
Empathy
Respect
Equality
Autonomy
Worth
Honor
Self-esteem
Recognition
Integrity.

CITATIONS

"Dignity: Its History and Meaning" by Michael Rosen (2012)

Kirchhoffer, David (2015). Personhood and human dignity. In Jānis T. Ozoliņš & Joanne Grainger (eds.), Foundations of Healthcare Ethics: Theory to Practice. Cambridge: (2015)

"The Concept of Human Dignity in Human Rights Discourse" by William Sweet (2012)

"Dignity: A History" by Charles A. L. Jr. (2017)

"Human Dignity and Bioethics: Essays Commissioned by the President's Council on Bioethics" edited by Adam Schulman and Robert P. George (2008)

"Human Dignity and the Foundations of International Law" by Patrick Capps (2014)

Dignity, Human (2002). An Ethical Inquiry. In Ellen Frankel Paul, Fred Dycus Miller & Jeffrey Paul (eds.), Bioethics. Cambridge University Press.

Atlan, Henri ; Knowledge, Glory & Dignity, On Human (2007). Knowledge, Glory and `On Human Dignity'. Diogenes 54 (3):11-17.

These sources provide a wealth of information and analysis on the historical, philosophical, legal, and practical aspects of the concept of dignity.

BOOKS BY THIS AUTHOR

Philosophy And Transcendence: The Life And Works Of Giovanni Pico Della Mirandola

"Philosophy and Transcendence" is a captivating exploration of the life and works of Giovanni Pico della Mirandola, a Renaissance philosopher whose ideas challenged the traditional views of his time. This book delves deep into Pico's transformative power of knowledge and his belief in personal and spiritual growth, and how these ideas influenced his works on philosophy, theology, and mysticism. Through a comprehensive analysis of his major works such as "Oration on the Dignity of Man" and "900 Theses," the reader will be taken on a journey of intellectual discovery, exploring Pico's views on the human condition, the role of God in the universe, and the transformative power of knowledge. With its engaging prose and insightful analysis, "Philosophy and Transcendence" is a must-read for anyone interested in the Renaissance period and the evolution of philosophical thought.

9 798390 055588